AFTER THE
Acceptance Letter

Seven Healthy Mindsets
for Emotional Wellness in College

Gina Davis, PsyD

Published by Rosered

Copyright © 2020 by Gina Davis, PsyD

All rights reserved. No part of this publication may be reproduced, distributed or transmitted in any form or by any means, including photocopying, recording, or other electronic or mechanical methods, without the prior written permission of the publisher, except in the case of brief quotations embodied in critical reviews and certain other noncommercial uses permitted by copyright law.

Neither the publisher nor the author are engaged in rendering professional advice or services to the individual reader. The ideas, procedures, and suggestions contained in this book are not intended as a substitute for consulting with your physician or mental health provider. All matters regarding your health require medical supervision. Neither the author nor the publisher shall be liable or responsible for any loss or damage allegedly arising from any information or suggestion in this book.

While the author has made every effort to provide accurate telephone numbers and Internet addresses at the time of publication, neither the publisher nor the author assume any responsibility for errors, or for changes that occur after publication. Further, the publisher does not have any control over and does not assume any responsibility for author or third-party websites or their content.

For permission requests, write to the author, at:

Gina Davis, PsyD
P.O. Box 11039
Oakland, CA 94611
gina@ginadavispsyd.com

After the Acceptance Letter: Seven Healthy Mindsets for Emotional Wellness in College/ Gina Davis, PsyD. —1st ed.

ISBN 978-1-953449-17-7

*To the young adults beginning
or continuing their mental health journeys.
Your courage will change the world.*

Contents

Preface: 7

Healthy College Mindset #1:
Yes, I "need" college, but colleges also need me. 11

Healthy College Mindset #2:
I will work to make my college experience
"good enough." 24

Healthy College Mindset #3:
College is a time to learn about myself. I don't have to
have it all figured out. 29

Healthy College Mindset #4:
I will mindfully choose which opportunities to pursue,
letting my values guide me. 36

Healthy College Mindset #5:
I'm an adult now, and adults ask for help when
they need it. 44

Healthy College Mindset #6:
Learning How to Take Care of My Mental Health Now Will Help
Me for the Rest of My Life 54

Healthy College Mindset #7:
College is an opportunity to practice building healthy
relationships. 76

Closing 86

Resources. 88

About the Author 93

Preface:

*"An overachiever walked into a bar.
Apparently, it wasn't set high enough."*

UNKNOWN

This book is for the kids who sacrificed their teenage years to the altar of getting accepted to college—the ones who spent their youth feeding their GPAs instead of their souls. It's for the young people (the new generation of college students) who maybe had a lot of guidance around school and grades and the college application process, but less support around finding out who they are, what they need, and what makes them a happy, well-adjusted human being.

I was one of those kids. I was destined to go to college since my conception. My parents say they used to stand over my crib when I was a baby and murmur, "College before marriage...college before marriage..." Both of my parents were first-generation college students. I was expected to excel, attend a "good school" at eighteen, and finish college in four years.

My path to college involved a lot of challenges. I'd attended public schools in Richmond, California through the fifth grade, but at the age of eleven, my parents enrolled me in a competitive, academically rigorous private school on financial aid, and I struggled for the next seven years. I struggled in math. I struggled in science. I struggled to learn French in the sixth grade when everyone around me had started in fourth. I'd spend every night working for hours on homework, while my private school peers seemed to breeze right through. But quitting simply wasn't an option. My parents and I knew that all this work and sacrifice had a purpose: so I could get into a good college.

I felt like I had to fight an uphill battle to get into a college I actually wanted to attend, but fight I did. I **believed** in the fight.

When I received an acceptance letter to my top-choice school, I cried tears of joy for the first time in my life. I'd worked my butt off, my family and I had sacrificed so much for so many years, and it had finally paid off.

Soon I found myself in New York City with my first fall semester starting, and all I could think was:

"Wait a second—I'm still the same person with the same insecurities as before?"

"Hold up—college isn't going to solve all my problems?"

"Wait a minute—you mean I still have to...like...work?"

(Regarding that last one: Of course I knew that college involved classes, tests, papers, and the like, but in all honesty, my brain hadn't quite wrapped itself around that yet.)

You see, I was so burned out from killing myself in order to get *into* college that I honestly hadn't put that much thought into the reality of being a college student. The focus on simply getting accepted was so intense that—for me personally, at least—I focused way more on getting into college during my teenage years than I did on, well, being a teenager. I was not the type of kid who hung out with her friends at the mall, didn't care about school or grades and was content to just exist and, you know, "be a kid." Instead, I was studying and cramming like a madwoman, trying to figure out how I could best position myself to be viewed in a positive light by the people who had power over me and my future. I didn't know anything else.

College is sold to kids like you as **The** Holy Grail. It's the "I'll be happy when" of your teenage years. And it's only one of many dreams that will be sold to you throughout your lifetime. After college it'll be, "I'll be happy when I get my first job." "I'll be happy when I finish grad school." "I'll be happy when I can afford a real vacation." "I'll be happy when I get into a relationship or get married." "I'll be happy when I own a house." "I'll be happy when I have a family of my own." "I'll be happy when I pay off these student loans." The goal posts keep moving further away.

So you got accepted to college (or will in the near future). Congratulations! You've spent a long time working and waiting for this moment.

Now what?

Contrary to what everyone has told you or what you may have told yourself, college is not going to solve all of your problems. You will still have problems, old and new.

You are not a completely different person. Every aspect of your life is not going to fall into perfect place. If you considered yourself an Ugly Duckling in high school, college is not going to turn you into a swan. (At least not overnight. Sorry.)

If you were not "fine" before, you most certainly are not "fine" because a college has now accepted you.

Believe it or not, when I started college, I thought all of the above was more or less true. I had the Golden Ticket and the Chocolate Factory was mine, forever!

I was wrong. And when I realized I wasn't "home free," I felt very, very lost.

Turns out, I was not alone. Many of my peers expressed the same feelings about their college years. They lament that they feel they wasted their time. They confide that they put on a brave face in public, but were privately unhappy, heartbroken, lonely, or struggling with a variety of issues. They say they couldn't understand why they felt empty. Overwhelmed. Homesick. Out of place. Unprepared. Scared. After all, they'd gotten everything they were supposed to want.

As a kid who played the get-into-college game and as a clinical psychologist who has worked in multiple college settings and with numerous high school and college-aged individuals over the years, I see people feeling, thinking, and doing the same things I did. I wrote this book because I want to be the voice that speaks to the real person who has to keep on living life after they've gotten their so-called Golden Ticket. I wanted to write the book I wish I'd had at eighteen. I can't say if I would have actually **heeded** the advice in these pages, but if I did, I hope that it would have saved me from a lot of self-blame, feeling lost about who I was and what I wanted, and expecting too much of myself. It would have freed me to do the one thing I *couldn't* do as a teenager: just be myself.

You've gotten into college. It's like you've been waiting in front of a door, working to figure out the secret password. You finally cracked it! The door has opened.

Now you have to walk inside and begin your personal college journey. The work of becoming a person. The work of becoming *you*.

HEALTHY COLLEGE MINDSET #1:

Yes, I "need" college, but colleges also need me.

"The most common way people give up their power is by thinking they don't have any."

ALICE WALKER, WRITER

"I got into college!" I exclaimed. It was Christmas Eve, and I was sitting at a dining table with my cousins, about to dig into our annual family dinner.

No one said anything. Least of all "congratulations." It was total silence. Crickets.

"It was my first choice," I added, trying to nudge some kind of response out of them.

I didn't understand this reaction (or lack thereof) to my news. Didn't they realize how hard I had worked for this? What a big deal this was for me? How I'd spent the past four years of high school—no, my entire life—working towards this?

"Just remember, Gina. Even though you need to go to college, colleges also need students," one of my cousins replied gruffly.

Although my family's response wasn't the most encouraging, kind, or arguably appropriate thing to say to someone sharing a very meaningful accomplishment, in the years that followed, I found myself remembering those words again and again.

Colleges need students.

Just like supermarkets need shoppers, restaurants need diners, and Netflix needs subscribers.

And they need them for one thing: to make money. A college is a business. It takes money to employ professors, presidents, and provosts. Colleges have to pay rent, maintain the dormitories, stock their cafeterias with food, and pay the people who prepare it. It's a successful business if in spite of all these costs, it's turning a profit. That's where you come in.

Years later, when I worked in the Student Affairs department at a small college in San Francisco, I got to see the college game from the opposite side of the street. The people in Student Affairs liked to joke that our team was comprised of introverted helpers, while the Admissions team was comprised of extroverted sellers. It was Admissions' job to go out and sell the school to high school students and their parents, to convince them to buy.

Every college has an angle in terms of how they will market themselves to you. Some colleges, like cars, sell themselves. The Ivy Leagues sell themselves on prestige, exclusivity and reputation—like Mercedes Benz or Tesla. Other colleges sell from the career angle ("80 percent of our alums find employment right after graduation"), or the affordable angle ("a majority of our students receive partial or full scholarships"), or the location angle ("You'll be steps from the beach!"). There's also the sports angle, the personal empowerment angle, the lots-of-individual-attention angle, and the party school angle, to name just a few. No matter what kind of person you are, no matter what you care about, want out of life or out of a college experience, there is a college out there that is working to figure out exactly what you value and make sure you know enough about them to want to apply. All so they can, at some point, get your money.

I realize this sounds cynical, but it's simply how our country operates. Issues can arise, however, when you're a teenager and everyone around you is saying you simply *have* to buy the very best, sexiest, snazziest car you can afford. So you work your tail off and sacrifice and fret and sweat and wring your hands along with all your other classmates and you don't question what you're told ("Everybody's doing it, so it must be right!") or even stop long enough to examine your own values and needs...and you don't realize until too late that you've been asking the wrong questions.

In high school, the question on everyone's mind is, "Will I get into a good college?"

When maybe a better question would be, "Why do *I* want to go to college?"

Now, I know what you're gonna say, "Um, I want to go to college because I have to! Everyone needs a college degree these days. In fact, a college degree is small potatoes. You really have to go to graduate school if you want to have a comfortable life." I'm not disputing the value of a college degree itself. What I am disputing, however, is the approach I see in high school students who put most or all of the focus on the accomplishment of getting accepted and not enough of the focus on themselves. Yes, you are the senior class president, the leader of your community service club, a straight-A-making, bake-sale-cookie-baking, fun-forsaking, acceptance-letter-raking machine...

...But you are also a person. As in human being. Human beings don't need to have their entire lives mapped out at eighteen. Some people just aren't ready to go to college at that age. Some don't go the college route at all and choose other paths.

So aside from the fact that's it's "necessary", why do *you* want to go to college?

Is it because you want to make new friends? Fall in love? Study creative writing? Get a job? Party harder than ever? Play ice hockey? Join a fraternity? Pay as little tuition as possible? Make career contacts? Live in a certain city?

This brings us to our first exercise.

A Quick Note about the exercises in this book: I realize that many of you may be reading this book electronically, so I've set up a free digital workbook with all the exercises on my website. Go to: www.ginadavispsyd.com/college to have the workbook emailed to you.

When completing these exercises, I want you to (always!) try to be as honest with yourself as you can. This book and the exercises in it are about you – the real you. Not the persona you present to the world, not the narrative your personal statement reads, and not the person your parents, friends, or teachers think you should be. Don't think too hard and don't overanalyze. Just try to be honest.

Also, if you need more space to write your answers, make it (notebook, Notes app, etc.):

What I Want to Get Out of College:

What were some of the best things about high school?

What were some of the worst/hardest things about high school?

How do you want your college experience to be different from your high school experience?

What do *you* want to get out of college?

When you graduate, what will have made the experience worth it?

What do you need from a college experience to feel good about these years after they're over?

Sometimes people get caught up in the "shoulds" when it comes to choosing their college path: "I *should* go to the most selective school I can possibly get into." "I *should* go to the school that offered me the free ride, even though money isn't an issue and I don't. Actually. Want. To. Go. There." "I *should* go to Brown because it's the most prestigious college I got into, and that's what everybody expects me to do." "I *should* go to State because it's close to home, even though it doesn't offer the major I want." Is this happening to you? Are you *should*-ing on yourself?

My Self-Care Needs

Next, we're going to explore the things you need in order to take care of yourself in college, i.e. self-care in college. Common areas of self-care include, but are not limited to: physical self-care, psychological self-care, social-emotional self-care, spiritual self-care, financial self-care, social self-care and academic/professional self-care.

Go through each section and jot down a few words. If you already know where you're going to college, use this exercise as a place to write about how you will ensure your self-care needs are met at your future school/location:

Physical: (ex: What kind of setting do I do my best work in? Do I want to be close to home? How does the weather factor in? What about the food options? What things do I need at this college/new town in order to meet my physical health needs?)

Psychological: (ex: Does the school have the mental health resources I need? Are the students happy? Will I have the space I need for alone/quiet time?)

Social-Emotional: (ex: Will I be able to find comforting activities, people, places and relationships? Can I get involved in my college community in a way that is meaningful to me?)

_____

_____

_____

_____

_____

_____

_____

Spiritual: (ex: Do I already have a spirituality that I can continue to explore in college? Am I looking for a spiritual or religious community? Do I want to be able to spend time alone for self-reflection, or in nature?

_____

_____

_____

_____

_____

_____

_____

Financial: (ex: How will I finance my education and how much am I willing to spend? Will I have enough money to do things I enjoy in addition to paying for school? Do I understand the real-life implications of taking out student loans?)

_____

_____

_____

_____

_____

_____

_____

Academic/Professional: (ex: What is a good fit for me in terms of educational and academic challenge? How will what I study relate to a possible career path?)

_____

_____

_____

_____

_____

_____

_____

If there is an area of self-care that was not included above that you want to add, please do so below:

_____

_____

_____

_____

_____

_____

_____

_____

Going to college is a perfectly fine idea, but an even better idea is knowing how to choose the college experience that will be right for *you*. Always remember that underneath the grades, the accomplishments, and the SAT scores, you're still a person. You're the one who has to actually, you know, go to college, to live with the reality of this decision every day, to do the hard work.

And you are not a robot. Quite the opposite. You have needs, feelings, values, desires.

And you matter.

HEALTHY COLLEGE MINDSET #2:

I will work to make my college experience "good enough."

"The best is the enemy of the good."

VOLTAIRE, PHILOSOPHER

It was the summer before college started and I was at a doctor's appointment.

"Are you excited about starting school in New York?" Dr. L asked.

"Yes! I'm a little nervous, but so, so excited!"

"I think you're going to like it."

"Of course I will!" I practically bellowed. "I mean, it's college! The best years of your life!"

He paused and looked down at the floor. He seemed to be arguing with himself internally.

"Well," he said gently. "Maybe not the *best* years of your life…"

I looked at him like he had suddenly grown a second head. He must have noticed my facial expression, because he started explaining himself, talking about how he'd had the same mindset when he was eighteen and, quite frankly, had a better time in graduate school than undergrad.

But by that point I wasn't listening. Like I said earlier on, getting into college was my own personal Holy Grail. Who cared about the haters who tried to rain on my parade? How dare they attempt to dampen my feverish enthusiasm?

Dr. L wasn't the only one trying to get me to come back down to earth in terms of my astronomical expectations. At first-year convocation, one of the deans gave a speech in which she said (paraphrasing): "The college years can be great years, but don't pressure yourself to make them The Best Years of Your Life. Hopefully, you'll have many years of joy and excitement and happiness ahead of you. And wouldn't it be sad if it was all downhill from here?"

There is a mythos around college being "the best years of your life." It's a very American mythos, I think. Like Johnny Appleseed, Davy Crockett, or the concept of "having it all." But the mythos about college being the best years of your life is also about as real as the Headless Horseman.

Believe me, I am not trying to rain on your parade, either. I want you to go to college and have an amazing time. I want your expectations exceeded! I want ALL of your wildest college dreams to come true and then some!

But if that doesn't happen, I want you to be okay. That's why I wrote this book.

If you succumb to the pitfalls of super-high expectations, you are likely setting yourself up for disappointment and disillusionment. Just because the college years *can* be some of the best years of your life, doesn't mean they *have* to be. You've probably heard the expression that expectations are just disappointments in disguise. I'm not telling you to not set any expectations at all, but I am telling you to make them reasonable. Very reasonable.

For people who are used to pushing themselves really hard, this can be difficult to do. Your "lowered" version of your expectations may still be, well, pretty high. So set them even lower. Make them even smaller. Make them so reasonable that you raise an eyebrow at yourself. Why? Because anything that happens beyond that becomes icing on the cake.

Instead of reaching for The Best Years of My Life or Bust, try instead for The Good Enough Years of My Life. Because good enough is good enough.

Expectations Revisited

On the left side, list out your Best Years of Your Life expectations, and in the right column, revise them to be scaled way, way, way back.

For example:

"I'm gonna make so many friends!" → "I hope to meet some really cool people and come out of this with a few lasting friendships."

"I'm gonna triple major, I just know I can do it!" (Yes, there was a time when I was telling myself this.) → I know generally what I want to study. I'll take a few classes in those areas and decide my direction once I have more information. One major is fine."

"College is gonna be best years of my life!" → "College has the potential to be a fruitful and fun experience for me."

Now you try:

Best Years of My Life!	Good Enough Revision:

Remember that college is just one season of your life. Hopefully you will live to see many more years, to experience the long life ahead of you. It sounds strange to think about now, but one day you'll look back on college and you'll be 35. Or 50. Or 90.

Years of life are just that...years...of life. And as we all know, life is never perfect. But that doesn't mean it can't be good enough.

HEALTHY COLLEGE MINDSET #3:

College is a time to learn about myself. I don't have to have it all figured out.

"Be brave. Take risks. Nothing can substitute experience."

PAULO COELHO, NOVELIST

There was a show on MTV when I was a teenager called *Made*. Real kids from all over the country would contact the producers of the show and share their big dreams: "I want to be made into a rock star." "I want to be made into a beauty queen." "I want to be made into a cheerleader." "I want to be made into a singer." "I want to be made into a basketball champion." You get the idea.

The selected kids (usually high school students) would be assigned a personal "Made Coach" and begin some kind of rigorous training regime. They'd quickly realize they were in way over their heads, cry a lot, experience numerous crises of confidence, get pumped up and/or yelled at by their coaches, and in the end, make their dream come true. They would be *made*. More or less.

As you can probably guess, I was a big fan of this show when it first aired. I mean, it practically epitomized my high school achievement mindset! The mindset that said, "Once I become or do XYZ, I'll be happy. When my dream comes true, I'll be happy. I'll be made."

As cheesy as it might sound, I wanted college to be my Made. I wanted it to transform me into the person I always wanted to be. I thought it had the power to do that. But the truth is, college won't necessarily change you. You can work on changing yourself, but even then, change won't always manifest in the exact ways you want, plan, or expect. And it won't necessarily happen on your timeline.

I wish someone had told me that that I didn't have to be "made," do everything "right," that I was fine just as I was and regardless of what my ego or imagination told me, and that even when I felt like I wasn't doing enough, I was exactly where I was supposed to be. It's possible someone did tell me this, but I didn't listen. So I want to share this with you now and I hope that, unlike me, you can take what I have to say to heart: instead of approaching college as this magic lamp that must completely overhaul who you are, try to think of it more as a huge opportunity to learn about yourself. The better you know yourself, the more choices you can make that align with who that person is, wants, and needs. And that is a skill that will aid you tremendously throughout life.

Make learning about yourself a top priority during your college years. A common example is the roommate situation. One way people can learn about themselves is to live with other people. Your roommate experience might be great, horrible, or somewhere in between. I myself had a roommate for the first two years of college, and the experience had its ups and downs. It taught me that there were some aspects of living with another person that I really liked, and some I really didn't. More importantly, it taught me about my own preferences and needs with regards to living with others. It gave me more insight into who *I* was.

Hopefully, you have already done some of the work of learning about who you are, and college can be a bountiful continuation of that. But if you were like me and put all that "personal stuff" on the back-burner up until this point, now's your chance to put some experimental feelers out there and start the exciting work of figuring out who you are.

What Have I Already Learned About Myself?

Fill out the first section with any adjectives you feel are accurate, and include a few details:

Example: I am a <u>thrifty</u> person. Elaborate: <u>I reuse Ziploc bags, shop at thrift stores, and never eat out.</u>

I am a _____ person.

Elaborate:

_____

_____

_____

I am a _____ person.

Elaborate:

_____

_____

_____

I am a _____ person.

Elaborate:

_____

_____

_____

I am a _____ person.

Elaborate:

_____

_____

_____

I am a _____ person.

Elaborate:

_____

_____

_____

I am a _____ person.

Elaborate:

_____

_____

_____

What are some opportunities in college that can help me learn even more about myself?

Opportunity

_____

_____

What It Could Teach Me:

_____

_____

Opportunity

_____

_____

What It Could Teach Me:

_____

_____

Opportunity

_____

_____

What It Could Teach Me:

_____

_____

Opportunity

_____

_____

What It Could Teach Me:

_____

_____

Opportunity

_____

_____

What It Could Teach Me:

_____

_____

Opportunity

_____

_____

What It Could Teach Me:

_____

_____

The main point I want you to take away from this chapter is that college is not the finish line; it's just another lap of the race. Sure, it may be irksome to think that you haven't "arrived" yet (especially because that's why our society sells college acceptance as), but the good news is that arriving is not what life is actually about. Life, as corny and cliché as it sounds, is about the journey. You don't have to have it all figured out now that you're a college student. The truth is, you're just getting started on your adventure. The possibilities are endless, and the self-imposed pressure to have it all figured out on day one is optional.

HEALTHY COLLEGE MINDSET #4:

I will mindfully choose which opportunities to pursue, letting my values guide me.

"The talent is in the choices."

ROBERT DENIRO, (THE GREATEST) ACTOR (EVER)

Having just spoken about approaching college as a smorgasbord of opportunities to learn about yourself, I am now going to talk about the importance of choosing **which** opportunities you want to explore. There will be many to choose from.

It was a few days before fall semester started my first year, and my family and I were exploring my new neighborhood of Morningside Heights in New York City. We wandered into a nonprofit (the name must have intrigued one of us, though I can't remember it now). We were greeted by a nice man who told us about his work and the mission of the non-profit, and I told him I was about to start school up the street.

"Make sure you take advantage of all the opportunities that school has to offer," were his parting words to me.

Well, I took those words seriously—maybe a little *too* seriously. When school started, I was like a kid in a candy store. I signed up for tons of clubs and activities—everything from gospel singing to sign language. I feverishly said "yes" to everything—every invitation, every extra-curricular that even mildly piqued my interest, every chance I got to do or try something new.

I'm proud to say I was so enthusiastic, but the truth is you can't do everything. At least not well. Trying to take advantage of every opportunity that comes your way is, unfortunately, a one way ticket to burnout, exhaustion, and feeling like you're failing at life.

If you are reading this book, about to apply to college or have already gotten in, I'm going to take a guess that you are probably a pretty goal-oriented, can-do, go-to-it type of person. This can be a great thing, but it can also be a bit of a double-edged sword.

This is why it's so important to make your choices with mindfulness. In a nutshell, mindfulness is the practice of being fully present with whatever is happening right now, with gentleness, compassion, and non-judgement. Contrary to what some may believe, mindfulness is not:

Telling yourself things are fine when they're not (like that ever works!)

Getting rid of your thoughts

Getting rid of your feelings

Zoning out

Noticing and observing are two key facets of mindfulness. Your fevered mind may tell you that you have to do everything, but that doesn't mean you have to. You can notice the thoughts, the impulses, the feelings, and choose—with mindfulness—not to act on them.

Maybe it's because I went to college in New York City, but it seemed like there were a million things to do all the time. In fact, there probably were. Instead of mindfully choosing the ones that were important to me, the ones aligned with my values and realistic capacity, I initially took the route of "doing it all." Apparently, this is a trap a lot of people fall into. The issue is that often when you feel like to have to do it all, it's coming from a fear-based place. Some call it FOMO (fear of missing out).

Interestingly enough, doing nothing (the opposite) also tends to come from a fear-based place. For example, like many college students, I started college initially planning to study abroad during my junior year. But by the middle of my second year, I was no longer so enthusiastic about the idea. Maybe it was a by-product of overextending myself my first year combined with fear of the unknown, but I'd actually decided not to study abroad.

Then, as it sometimes does, fate intervened. I was traveling home for the holidays my sophomore year, making a connecting flight at the Dallas-Fort Worth airport. While waiting at the gate for my flight to San Francisco, a woman in her mid-twenties named Lauren started talking to me. She worked in New York City and was also flying home to the Bay Area for Christmas. Lauren asked me if I planned to study abroad next year, and I told her that I'd pretty much decided against it.

Well, that was not the answer that Lauren wanted to hear. From that point on, it became her single-minded mission to get me to change my mind. Lauren had studied abroad in Italy when she was in college, and was totally convinced I would regret not taking advantage of this particular opportunity. We sat and talked for a long time; she showed me pictures from her semester abroad on her digital camera, told enthralling stories, and basically convinced me that this was an opportunity I could not afford to pass up.

I never saw or talked to Lauren again, but by the time we landed in San Francisco, her campaign to get me to study abroad had planted a seed that later motivated me to take action. The following year, I studied abroad in Strasbourg, France, lived with an amazing host family, made lifelong friends, and— having never been out of the country before—had an incredible time. I was able to fully immerse myself in the experience, and it was one that influenced me more deeply than being superficially involved in a bazillion clubs. It scares me to think that fear and burnout almost prevented me from having this priceless experience.

I'm not telling you that you **have** to study abroad like I did (though I will tell you that all of my friends who opted out now say they regret it). Like college, studying abroad is not going to be a perfect experience. It's absolutely going to come with its own sets of challenges and setbacks, but it is another experience that can expand your horizons and teach you about yourself. My chance meeting and conversation with Lauren (okay, it was more like a brainwashing session) made me realize that my previous decision to not study abroad was based in fear: fear of being in a new country so far away from my usual surroundings where people spoke a different language, fear of meeting new people, and possibly feeling discomfort. Being afraid of those things wasn't wrong in and of itself, in fact, it was normal. But I was and am also a person who values having new experiences, personal growth, and courage to take healthy risks. So I went for it.

How do you know when a choice or decision is coming from a fear-based place? Mindfulness can be a first step in helping you figure it out. One of the great things about mindfulness is that it aspires to let all your thoughts and feelings exist without trying to change or judge them. Dr. Russ Harris, the creator of Acceptance Commitment Therapy (ACT) talks about the importance of letting your thoughts and feelings exist while still making choices that align with your values. Your values are what you value. They can be things like family, security, creativity, expression, honesty, freedom, loyalty, adventure, compassion and kindness.

In college, and in life, there are so many opportunities presented to you. Figuring out what to say no to is just as—if not more—important as knowing what to say yes to. Sometimes we have to make some tough decisions. Exploring and articulating our values, in addition to using mindfulness, can help guide us to the choices that work best for us.

My Values

Take a look at the values bank below. Circle your top five values. This bank is by no means exhaustive. If you don't see your value(s) on this list, add them in.

THE VALUES BANK

Flexibility · Determination · Sharing · Competence
Balance · Love · Compassion · Humor · Strength
Thrift · Trust · Honesty · Sincerity · Security · Wisdom
Expression · Originality · Health · Happiness · Intimacy
Friendship · Leadership · Mindfulness · Innovation
Cooperation · Responsibility · Empathy · Excellence
Exploration · Fairness · Dependability · Boldness · Beauty
Drive · Confidence · Spirituality · Family · Gratitude
Imagination · Belonging · Balance · Control
Enthusiasm · Bravery · Kindness · Helpfulness · Respect
Pragmatism · Justice · Self-Sufficiency · Loyalty · Courage
Resilience · Risk · Ambition · Self-esteem · Reason · Focus
Growth · Leisure · Patience · Financial Stability · Popularity
Fun · Directness · Service · Acceptance · Passion · Generosity
Discovery · Learning · Inquisitiveness · Fitness · Joy
Hard Work · Carefulness · Faith · Beauty · Decisiveness
Originality · Sensitivity · Skill · Creativity

Next, elaborate on your top five. How do you live these values on a day to day basis? How might you apply these values to your choices in college? Are you currently making choices that could stand to be more aligned with them?

Example: "My #1 value is creativity. I live this value by making time every day to work on my art."

My #1 value is

_____

I live this value by

_____

In college, I will live this value by:

_____

_____

My #2 value is

_____

I live this value by

_____

In college, I will live this value by:

_____

_____

My #3 value is

_____

I live this value by

_____

In college, I will live this value by:

_____

_____

My #4 value is

_____

I live this value by

_____

In college, I will live this value by:

_____

_____

My #5 value is

_____

I live this value by

_____

In college, I will live this value by:

_____

_____

Another example of using mindfulness and your values to choose which opportunities to pursue is the issue of student loans. You may value going to a good school no matter the cost, but you might also value saving money and not going into debt. Which value drives you more strongly and why? Can you find a way to compromise? Can you make a choice that aligns with your values and be happy (or at least live) with the outcome?

The practice of making values-based decisions with mindfulness is another skill that will help invaluably through the rest of adulthood. But if you still find yourself stuck or waffling in uncertainty, it can also be helpful to know when and how to ask for external guidance, which I'll discuss in the next chapter.

HEALTHY COLLEGE MINDSET #5:

I'm an adult now, and adults ask for help when they need it.

*"Ask for help not because you're weak,
but because you want to remain strong."*

LES BROWN, MOTIVATIONAL SPEAKER

If you're reading this book, you are probably quite familiar with the resources that have been set up to get you *into* college. Now it's time to switch the focus to the resources set up to get you *through* college.

When I started college, I really didn't realize how many resources were available on campus, placed there expressly for the purpose of helping me succeed (aka: graduate in four years). In addition to my advisor, there were deans for every single class. There was also the Dean of Studies, the Dean for International Students, the Transfer Advising Dean, the Dean of Student Success, the Dean of Study Abroad, and the Dean of Academic Assistance, to name a few.

In addition to the deans, my college had a counseling center, residential life (including many Resident Assistants, aka RAs), a writing center, a crisis hotline, disability/accessibility services, career development, primary care health services and academic support (i.e. tutoring). They even had a room you could reserve with sunlight lamps to treat Seasonal Affective Disorder (SAD).

When I worked as the Accessibility Specialist of a college, I was a member the Student Affairs team, which at that point consisted of myself, the Dean of Students, the Assistant Dean of Students, career services, residential life, counseling, and global programs (i.e. study abroad). The Student Affairs team met weekly with key members of Academic Affairs to discuss students of concern who might need additional support in order to, as we said: "Get across that stage and graduate." Combined, we called ourselves the Student Success and Advocacy Team.

So in case you were wondering: yes, you're being watched by your college's administration. I worked at and attended relatively small schools that had a lot invested in getting students to graduate, so the extent to which you are being watched will differ depending on the administration at your college or university. Some colleges take a more "sink-or-swim" approach with their students and let them muddle through on their own without much guidance or support, some are super involved and hands-on, and many fall somewhere in the middle. Depending on the person you are and the kind of support you know you need, you may want to consider this factor when choosing a college.

Regardless of which school you attend, you can be pretty sure that there will be the same basic lineup of resources available to you: mental health, tutoring, study abroad, residential life, disability services, and general academic counseling.

One thing I learned from working in Student Affairs is that college students are not always the best at asking for help, especially from the people whose job it is to provide it. One example of this comes from my friend, Deb, who openly admitted to her strong aversion to getting support from her college's disability services office. Deb had been tested and diagnosed with a learning disability in high school, and was eligible to receive accommodations in college (some common examples of disability accommodations include: longer times for taking tests, getting to record class lectures, getting to register for classes early), but she didn't want to use them. Her college's Disability Services office contacted her time and time again. The following is a paraphrased sample of their back and forth:

Disability Services: "Would you like to set up an appointment to come in and talk about our services?"

Deb: "No. F*ck off."

Disability Services: "Are you sure? We'd really like to talk with you about how our services can provide accommodations to help you succeed in college."

Deb: "No. F*ck off."

Disability Services: "But..."

Deb: "No. F*ck off."

Of course, it's completely your prerogative to choose if and when to ask for help. But keep this in mind: you've "hired" your school to give you an education, but you've also hired them to help you *complete* that education. Fortunately, most colleges have wised up to the fact that college students aren't machines—they have personal challenges and struggles and pain points just like any other human being. You aren't going to get all A's if your clinical depression is making it impossible to get out of bed. You aren't going to pass Western Civ if you never really learned how to write an essay. You aren't going to get to study abroad if the global programs director isn't filing the necessary paperwork for you to take temporary leave from school. And you aren't going to have an equitable chance at succeeding academically if you don't get the disability accommodations you need and are legally entitled to.

Consider this as well: after college, there will be very few times in your adult life when a group of people (outside of say, your close family or friends) will care about helping you meet your goals. Adult life does not come equipped with someone to help you punch up your resume or cover letter (unless you pay them). Adult life does not include a person who will advocate and fight for your disability accommodations at work (unless you pay them). And adult life does not have a group of people sitting around a table at a weekly meeting reviewing your grades and issues and personal hardships, trying to figure out how to help you succeed (unless you can afford a personal think tank). College is one of the few times you'll have this kind of support at your fingertips, and the fact is you're already paying for it, so you might as well use it.

Mind you, asking for help isn't the same thing as getting someone else to do the work *for* you. We therapists are big believers in not doing things for others that they can and should do for themselves, partly because it just doesn't work! You can tell someone to stop engaging in harmful or destructive behaviors until you're blue in the face, but the commitment is ten thousand times more powerful when it comes internally. College is a time for you to learn how to take care of yourself, to learn that you *can* do things that seem intimidating, new, or challenging and with the support of a team of people who want to see you move across that graduation stage in four years. I am in no way telling you to show up at your Registrar's office, barking orders at them to build you the perfect class schedule. First of all, that's totally inappropriate, and second of all, they'd probably look at you confused and say, "Um. That's not my job." The resources on campus are there to support you and guide you in the right direction, but at the end of the day, you're the only one responsible for your life.

With that in mind, the following exercise will help you figure out your own relationship to asking for help and support from others.

Asking for Help

Example of a time I needed help in the past <u>and asked for it</u>:

Did I get the help I needed? What was the outcome?

Example of a time I needed help in the past <u>and didn't ask for it</u>:

Did I get the help I needed? What was the outcome?

_____

_____

_____

_____

_____

Another example of a time I needed help in the past:

_____

_____

_____

_____

_____

Did I ask for help? Circle one: YES / NO

If yes, why and how? If no, why not?

_____

_____

_____

_____

_____

Did I get the help I needed? What was the outcome?

_____

_____

_____

_____

What are my beliefs around asking for help?

_____

_____

_____

_____

_____

If you find it difficult or problematic to ask for help, what are the most challenging parts? How can you challenge and revise your beliefs around asking for help if they are negative (ex: "Asking for help makes me look/feel weak." → "Asking for help allows me a chance to get the support I need.")

If you are generally comfortable asking for help when you need it, reflect on the ways in which you may need to put this skill to practice in college:

How do you find out about the resources *your* school has to offer? Your first step is to simply gather information. Usually, you'll get a full review of all the resources during student orientation. In my experience, however, this tends to be information overload for overwhelmed first-years, and not all of it sticks. Before classes start, take an hour or two to explore your school's website (look for pages/sections on things like Student Services, Student Affairs, Counseling, or Support Services). Your school should also provide you with a physical or electronic Student Handbook that will list all the campus resources in the table of contents. If you're still in the process of choosing which college to attend, talk to some of the current students. Ask them about their honest experiences with the deans, Disability Services, and administration.

Your next step will be to engage, because that is where you will make connections that can benefit and provide even more valuable information. Email your counselor or advisor and introduce yourself. If you need disability accommodations, contact your school's office of disability or accessibility services, ideally at least a month before classes start **(see footnotes 1 & 2)**. Call the tutoring center and set up a time to stop by, simply to learn about what they offer and how it can help you. Make an appointment to see a therapist at the counseling center. Visit your professors during office hours. Check in with your RA.

It's okay to make mistakes. In fact, it's inevitable. It's also okay to be nervous about asking for help. Be afraid. Be reluctant. Be too proud or embarrassed or self-sufficient to ask, and then...do it anyway. Because you're an adult now, and adults ask for help when they need it.

Footnote 1: If you had an IEP (Individualized Education Plan) or 504 Plan in high school, it was your school's responsibility to ensure that your disability accommodations were implemented. In college, the Americans with Disabilities Act (1990) still applies, but colleges won't proactively give you accommodations or schedule an IEP meeting. You are responsible for connecting with disability services and letting them know what you need.

Footnote 2: Disability is defined by the Americans with Disabilities Act (1990) as: "a physical or mental impairment that substantially limits one or more major life activities, a person who has a history or record of such an impairment, or a person who is perceived by others as having such an impairment." Students living with mental health conditions (ex: anxiety disorders, bipolar disorder, post-traumatic stress disorder, major depressive disorder) and students in recovery from substance abuse or addiction may be protected under the ADA and eligible to receive disability accommodations if the aforementioned criteria are met. Contact the Disability Services office at your school to learn more.

HEALTHY COLLEGE MINDSET #6:

Learning How to Take Care of My Mental Health Now Will Help Me for the Rest of My Life

"My recovery from manic depression has been an evolution, not a sudden miracle."

PATTY DUKE, ACTOR & HEALTH ADVOCATE

By the end of my first year in college, I was pretty depressed. As you can probably guess, all those years of buildup and promise, the stock and faith I'd put into college being my Holy Grail, my Golden Ticket, my MTV Made, had resulted in an inevitable letdown. I'd had an idea of who I was supposed to be, how that person was supposed to feel, think and act, and I felt like I was failing at being that person and it was all my fault. Looking back, I wish I had cut myself a huge break. So many amazing, fun, cool things had happened. I'd had fun, made lots of new friends, and I had grown in many ways. But because it didn't look exactly the way I'd envisioned in my idealizing, fantasizing, romanticizing brain, I told myself I was messing up.

College is a time when many mental health issues can surface. For many people, it is their first time living away from home.

Freedom can be liberating, but it can also feel overwhelming and intense. Young people can experience their first psychotic break or manic episode when moving away from home for the first time, which coincides with the college years for many. Depression, anxiety, relationship issues, academic pressure, financial stressors, substance abuse, trouble transitioning to college and dealing with past and current traumas are common issues that have presented in the college students I've worked with.

We cannot receive help if we don't ask for it, but we cannot ask for help if we don't know we need it. College students don't always know themselves well enough to be able to identify when they're struggling emotionally—this is part of the personal learning curve that comes from this experience. As with everything else, learning to take care of your mental health is a skill.

Let's start by reflecting on what you know about your mental health so far. This exercise will prompt you to reflect on your past experiences with common mental health issues (though the issues listed below are in no way exhaustive), how they impacted you, and how you coped:

My Mental Health Journey So Far

Have you had experiences of feeling anxious, panicked, or struggled with uncontrollable worry? If so, share a little about them here. You don't have to write more than you are comfortable.

How these feelings impacted my thoughts/feelings/behavior:

How you coped (ex: talked to someone, drank more, denied my feelings, lashed out):

_____

_____

_____

_____

_____

_____

_____

On a scale of 0-10, 0 been "not effective at all" and 10 being "extremely effective", how would you rate the healthiness and efficacy of these coping behaviors?

1 2 3 4 5 6 7 8 9 10

Have you have had experiences of feeling sad or depressed? If so, share a little about them here. You don't have to write more than you are comfortable.

How these feelings impacted my thoughts/feelings/behavior:

How you coped (ex: talked to someone, drank more, denied my feelings, lashed out):

___

On a scale of 0-10, 0 been "not effective at all" and 10 being "extremely effective", how would you rate the healthiness and efficacy of these coping behaviors?

1 2 3 4 5 6 7 8 9 10

Have you have had experiences of feeling that your anger was out of control, or you became aggressive? If so, share a little about them here. You don't have to write more than you are comfortable.

How these feelings impacted my thoughts/feelings/behaviors:

How you coped (ex: talked to someone, drank more, denied my feelings, lashed out):

___

On a scale of 0-10, 0 been "not effective at all" and 10 being "extremely effective", how would you rate the healthiness and efficacy of these coping behaviors?

1 2 3 4 5 6 7 8 9 10

Have you had deeply distressing or disturbing experiences that impacted you emotionally afterwards? If so, share a little about them here. You don't have to write more than you are comfortable.

_____

_____

_____

_____

_____

_____

How these feelings impacted my thoughts/feelings/behaviors:

_____

_____

_____

_____

_____

_____

_____

How you coped (ex: talked to someone, drank more, denied my feelings, lashed out):

_____

_____

_____

_____

_____

_____

_____

_____

On a scale of 0-10, 0 been "not effective at all" and 10 being "extremely effective", how would you rate the healthiness and efficacy of these coping behaviors?

1 **2** **3** **4** **5** **6** **7** **8** **9** **10**

Have you experienced periods of high stress (externally or internally applied)? If so, share a little about them here. You don't have to write more than you are comfortable.

How these feelings impacted my thoughts/feelings/behaviors:

How you coped (ex: talked to someone, drank more, denied my feelings, lashed out):

_____

_____

_____

_____

_____

_____

_____

On a scale of 0-10, 0 been "not effective at all" and 10 being "extremely effective", how would you rate the healthiness and efficacy of these coping behaviors?

1 2 3 4 5 6 7 8 9 10

The truth is, you already have ways of coping with challenging emotions and situations. One of the aims of therapy and mental health is to recognize whether your current coping mechanisms are helping you or hurting you. If your coping skills are underdeveloped or causing more damage than good, therapy can help you learn and apply healthier coping strategies.

It's important to be able to recognize the signs that your mental health needs some attention. This is another skill to be learned and sharpened. I call these "yellow" flags instead of "red flags" because they are earlier signs of trouble ahead. Yes, I'm biased, but I'm a big proponent of everyone going to therapy, even when there's nothing "wrong." The sooner you recognize a problem or potential issue, the easier and less costly it will be to address it. You don't wait until your car's completely falling apart before taking it to get repaired; you take it for regular tune ups and maintenance. You wouldn't wait until your ship is completely underwater before calling for a life raft. You want to try to catch yourself before the flags turn red.

My Mental Health Yellow Flags:

Given your existing experiences and how well you know yourself, what are some of the early signs that your mental health is struggling and needs attention?

Examples: *I start sleeping less (or oversleeping), I feel edgy for no apparent reason, I feel like crying all the time, my grades start slipping, I start to self-isolate, I start being self-critical, I eat less, I eat more, I blow up at people, I drink or use substances more frequently/ in higher quantities, I feel urges to use substances even when I know they're not good for me, I spend hours watching TV or scrolling through the internet mindlessly, I start having negative thoughts like "I'd be better off dead"*:

Early Warning Signs That I Am Not Okay Mentally/Emotionally.

1. _____
2. _____
3. _____
4. _____
5. _____
6. _____
7. _____
8. _____
9. _____
10. _____

Try to come up with at least five Yellow Flags. If you are having trouble completing this list, ask your close friends or family members who know you well for insight. Once you've completed it, keep this list within reach and refer to it often. You may discover new items to add to the list or find yourself revising it.

Once you get a handle on what your individual mental health yellow flags are (see above), you will want to have a set plan in place for how to respond when you recognize yellow flags popping up. Here, you'll re-list your yellow flags, name some healthy coping skills you can apply on your own first, list some people you can reach out to if the aforementioned coping skills don't result in you feeling better, and list some professionals/outside resources that you can always contact if none of the first steps work:

My Mental Health Action Plan

STEP ONE: Early Warning Signs That I Am Not Okay Mentally/Emotionally (REPEAT FROM ABOVE)

1. _____
2. _____
3. _____
4. _____
5. _____
6. _____
7. _____
8. _____
9. _____
10. _____

_____

_____

If any of these yellow flags are present or occurring, that's your cue to move on to STEP TWO:

STEP TWO: Self-Soothing Behaviors I can do <u>on my own</u> (examples: take a shower/bath, listen to music, watch an episode of my favorite show, eat some yummy food, take a walk, take a nap, write in my journal, do some stretches/exercise, meditate, make art)

_____

_____

_____

_____

_____

_____

If you've tried these self-soothing activities and are still not feeling better, move on to STEP THREE:

STEP THREE: Outside support

Three people I can reach out to for support (ex: friends, family members)

Name: _____
Phone #: _____

Name: _____
Phone #: _____

Name: _____

Phone #: _____

If you've called these people and you still aren't feeling better, or if the people you've listed are not available to talk to you, move on to STEP FOUR:

STEP FOUR: Professional Support

Mental Health hotlines in the United States, available 24/7/365:

1-800-SUICIDE

1-800-273-TALK

1-888-628-9454 (En Español)

1-800-799-4889 (for deaf or hard of hearing)

If you are having thoughts of hurting yourself, call 911 or go to your nearest emergency room.

A list of crisis hotlines is also included in the Resources section at the end of this book **(page 88)**

Keep your mental health action plan within reach and bookmark this page for easy access when needed.

**

Next, I'm going to talk about how to access mental health services (i.e. therapy) in college:

College/University Counseling centers: Most colleges have counseling centers that offer a fixed number of free sessions for students per academic year. Some colleges also offer Student Assistance Programs (SAPs) which allow students a limited number of sessions with an off-campus therapist. College counseling centers should have a list of mental health resources for you to use outside of the free sessions offered by the school, including local therapists who offer reduced (or, sliding scale) fees for students, upon request.

Health Insurance:

In-Network therapists: In most cases, if you're under 26 years old and covered by your parents' insurance, you can call your insurance company and obtain a list of in-network therapists in your area. In-network therapists will provide therapy sessions for a co-pay; the amount of which varies depending on your specific insurance plan.

Out-of-Network therapists: These are mental health providers that are not contracted with insurance companies (or not your specific health insurance company). You have to pay the therapist the full (or agreed-upon) fee up front. Again, depending on your health insurance plan, you may be able to get a partial refund on the fees paid to the therapist directly if you request a superbill at the end of each month from your therapist. A superbill is essentially a receipt stating the dates you met for sessions, the clinical diagnosis given to you by your therapist, and confirmation that you have paid your therapist directly for their services. The therapist will provide you with the superbill upon request, but you must submit the superbill to your insurance in order to receive partial reimbursement.

Call your insurance company to find out what your co-pay for an in-network therapist will be, and if your plan offers partial reimbursement for out-of-network mental health providers. Make sure to have your insurance card with you when you call.

Therapy Groups: Unfortunately, the cost of therapy can be prohibitive. One alternative to individual therapy is group therapy. Groups often meet weekly, and can be a place to learn new skills, get support and make positive connections for less than the cost of a typical therapy session. Your college may offer therapy groups based on different themes (ex: stress, men's issues, anxiety disorders). You may want to do an internet search, or ask the mental health counseling center at your school for group therapy referrals (i.e. recommendations).

Sliding Scale: As noted above, some therapists will offer clients a reduced fee depending on their financial situation. If you are doing research and come across a therapist you think you'd like to work with, don't be shy about contacting them and asking if they are currently offering sliding scale fees to college students.

Online therapy: Telehealth and tele-therapy are becoming more widely used, and they come with their own set of advantages and disadvantages. Be sure to ask questions and review the fine print in terms of what you'll be receiving. There are numerous online therapy platforms, some of which I'll list in the Resources section at the end of this book.

Suggestions for choosing a therapist: The number one thing I tell people who are looking for a therapist is: shop around. Don't feel that you have to stick with the first therapist you meet. All therapists have different approaches and styles. Some like to remain a silent blank slate and let you do most of the talking. Some are more interactive. Some assign homework and exercises and some don't. Some are open to disclosing certain details from their own lives if they feel it will benefit you and the session, and some keep their personal lives in a locked safe. And yes, some therapists can cause harm and are just not very good at what they do. If you feel weird or just don't click with the first (or second, or third) therapist you meet, it's okay. Keep looking and don't decide on one until you've spent some time sampling different therapists and their styles and approaches. I recommend trying two to three sessions with each therapist before making up your mind.

Ideally, you will go into a first therapy session knowing what you want to work on and have at least an idea of your therapy goals. Take some time before the session to jot down some notes if you need to refer to them later on. Be transparent about what you're looking for and need.

It can be helpful to ask your therapist about how they like to work. "Theoretical orientation" is the term the mental health profession uses to describe what method of therapy they apply. Some of common theoretical orientations in psychology today include person-centered, psychodynamic, mindfulness-based, cognitive behavioral therapy (CBT), solution-focused, attachment-based, multicultural, humanistic and eclectic (the latter means the therapist integrates a variety of theoretical approaches or techniques in their work). It is worthwhile to do some research on the differences to help you decide which style works best for you. You can simply ask your therapist: "What is your theoretical orientation?" and ask them to explain what it means to you and how it applies to their work with clients.

You may also want to inquire about how they've treated certain psychological issues in the past, how they conceptualize and would proceed with your own treatment if you continue to work together. A good question to ask yourself (and discuss with your therapist) is: "How will I know when my therapy goals have been attained?" "How would my life look different and how would I feel different?" "What is the evidence of change I'll look for?"

In addition, you'll want to interview your therapist about their experience working with any communities you identify with (i.e. race, gender, disability, sexuality). Their ability, or lack thereof, to conduct culturally competent therapy may be a deal maker, or a deal breaker.

I want to note here that there is a difference between feeling that you and a therapist are not a good fit and feeling discomfort in a therapy session. Starting therapy (for the first time or with someone new) can be an inherently uncomfortable experience. The majority of patients quit therapy after the first session. This is probably be due to a variety of reasons, including the unfortunate stigma that still surrounds mental health and illness, but my sense—having been both a therapist and a client—is that people have trouble managing the discomfort they feel in a therapy session. If it helps, feel free to name the discomfort you're experiencing in the room with your therapist. They won't (or shouldn't) judge you for feeling nervous. Expect a certain amount of initial discomfort, and don't expect it to fade overnight.

In that vein, I would also caution you to not expect therapy to fix your life overnight. With the therapy process, we say that things often feel like they get worse before they get better. It's not going to feel great talking about painful personal subjects, but if you commit to the process, put in the hard work and emotional heavy lifting, and keep showing up for yourself, the awkward/tough/painful period of therapy will usually, eventually give way to a more rewarding one.

Like taking care of your physical health, mental health is not something you "do" once and then are done with forever. You wouldn't go to one exercise class or eat one healthy meal and then say: "That's it. I'm good. I'm done for the rest of my life!" Similarly, you don't want to wait until you're fifty years old to begin the practice of learning how to take care of your body. Maintaining your physical health, as with maintaining your mental health, is an ongoing, lifelong process. Learning how to best nurture this part of yourself now will set you up for success for the rest of your life.

HEALTHY COLLEGE MINDSET #7:

College is an opportunity to practice building healthy relationships.

"You've got to learn to leave the table when love is no longer being served."

NINA SIMONE, MUSICIAN

In late 2012 I was fresh out of graduate school, and had moved from the San Francisco Bay Area to Los Angeles; I'd accepted a year-long postdoctoral fellowship at Mount St. Mary's University's Counseling and Psychological Services. Aside from my sister (who's lived in LA for years) and my new coworkers, I didn't know too many people there.

Amy and I had actually gone to college together (even graduated the same year), but we hadn't known one another at all as students. When I told one of our mutual friends about my move to Los Angeles, she introduced us via email. Amy was originally from LA, had returned to California after graduating, and now lived with her family, about twenty minutes from where I'd moved. We met and became friends almost instantly, and I had some of my most fun LA memories with her. She was always down to go on adventures! We would get together on the weekends and drive to Hermosa Beach, gorge ourselves on pho and go discount nail polish shopping in the San Gabriel Valley, eat French Dip sandwiches at Phillipe's in downtown LA, listen to live jazz at LACMA, and one time we even watched a movie at the Hollywood Forever Cemetery. She was one of those friends you instantly click and feel like you're on the same page with.

One day, we were on one of our outings when the topic of friendship came up. We were both now in our late twenties and had endured friendship losses and challenges over the years. We had both come to realizations about various friendships in our lives, most of which had started when we were younger (middle school, high school, college) and no longer seemed to quite fit. These were friendships that at one point or another had become stale, confusing, or even painful. At that time, I was still very much of the mindset that I had to not only accept but fight for any friendship that came my way, even if I was unhappy. I'd gone through earlier periods of my life where I felt alone, been treated like an outcast, and as a result figured that that in general, people didn't want to be my friend. I'd carried the "beggars can't be choosers" mentality into my twenties.

"You know," Amy said, "when you're young, you sometimes put up with bad behavior because you don't know any better, feel obligated to the other person, or don't think you can have something better. But we have the right to choose who we want in our lives."

When a friendship—or any other kind of relationship—is working, the experience is really different from when it's not. This is not to say of course that healthy friendships don't have their natural ups and downs, but cultivating and maintaining healthy relationships is yet another area of life that takes experience, learning, and applying the lessons learned.

Below is a chart I use in therapy to prompt a discussion about healthy relationships. Relationships (including romantic or sexual relationships, friendships, family and others) can exist on a spectrum from healthy to unhealthy to abusive. Review the chart below, then move on to the first exercise:

Healthy Relationships	**Unhealthy Relationships**	**Abusive Relationships**
Hallmarks: respect, good communication, trust, honesty, equality	**Hallmarks:** breaks in communication, pressure, dishonesty, struggles for control, inconsiderate behavior	**Hallmarks:** accusations, blame-shifting, isolation, pressure, manipulation
What it looks like: You make decisions together and can openly discuss issues, problems, conflicts, choices. You enjoy spending time together but can also be happy apart.	**What it looks like:** One person tries to make most decisions, may put pressure on the other person, or refuse to take responsibility for hurtful actions. You feel you should only spend time with this person.	**What it looks like:** One person makes all the decisions in the relationship (about choices, friends, boundaries, what is true and what isn't). You feel you cannot spend time with others, or talk to others about what is really happening in the relationship.

Adapted from The Relationship Spectrum" (Source: The Hotline)

Defining Healthy Relationships

How do you define healthy relationships? What parts of the chart struck you as most important in healthy relationships? Was there anything that you felt needed to be added? Revised? Take a few minutes to reflect:

What stood out to me about this chart:

Was there anything you didn't agree with? If yes what was it, and why?

My definition of a healthy relationship:

Because college is hopefully just one of many life chapters ahead, it's important to look back on what you've learned about healthy relationships so far. Complete the following exercise:

My Relationship History So Far

Do I have experience with healthy relationships? What did they feel like? How did I know they were healthy?

Do I have experience with unhealthy relationships? What did they feel like? How did I know they were unhealthy?

Do I have experience with relationships I thought were healthy but turned out to be unhealthy? How did I figure out they were unhealthy and what did I do?

Things I've Learned About Healthy Relationships So Far (ex: healthy relationships don't require that I always put my needs last):

More questions for relationship reflection:

Do I want my relationships in college and beyond to look/feel different from my high school relationships? If so, how?

How I will challenge myself to grow socially in college? (ex: I will not self-isolate, I will join a few clubs and be open to meeting new people, I will take a leadership role, I will introduce myself to people, I will say no to relationships that do not feel healthy or positive.)

What are my top five standards for healthy friendship or romantic relationship? (ex: mutual respect, trust, consistency) These are your deal breakers (i.e. if they're not present, you will keep it moving)

1.
2.
3.
4.
5.

How will you know when it's time to "leave the table when love is no longer being served" (i.e. remove yourself from a relationship when it is no longer positive or healthy)? (ex: I feel drained after spending time with a particular person, I don't feel like I can be myself in this relationship, I get blamed for things on a regular basis)

_____

_____

_____

_____

_____

_____

_____

We humans are social beings, and for that reason we need relationships. But we get to choose the relationships we let into our lives. Relationships can be a source of tremendous strength and joy, but they can also be damaging, hurtful or limiting. Listen to and respect your needs, and recognize that some relationships end and that's okay. Some of my most painful past relationships have taught me more about myself—and my strength—than the healthy ones. Contrary to what society tells us, a relationship does not have to last a lifetime in order for it to have been worthwhile, or at the very least, a chance for growth and personal discovery.

Closing

"Life itself is your teacher, and you are in a state of constant learning."

BRUCE LEE, MARTIAL ARTIST

I currently work as a therapist at a middle school, and one thing I tell the kids I work with is that middle school is your time to screw up, so that by the time you get to high school, you'll have a better handle on what you're doing. You'll have already been unable to open your locker in time to get to class...and learned from it. You'll have already flunked math...and learned from it. You'll already have been best friends with someone one day only to be on the receiving end of their betrayal the next...and learned from it. All of this growth, this failing and flailing around, is setting you up for high school, where, as they say: "things count." You are not failure as long as you have learned from your mistakes.

You've been through middle school and high school, and are about to enter a whole new chapter of your life, filled with its own lessons and many, many learning opportunities. Look back on the many things you've initially sucked at, improved at and maybe even eventually mastered. When you think about it, everything in life is learning. We all had to start somewhere.

I got my drivers' license when I was seventeen years old—a good year after almost all of my peers. I love driving now, but I wasn't a natural when I first started out. In fact, the first time my dad took me to practice in an empty Montgomery Ward's parking lot, he basically had a panic attack. Weeks and months went by, and I messed up time and time again. One time I drove the car up on the curb, and a man watching from across the street literally fell over laughing. You aren't always going to be great at something the first (or second, or third, or fiftieth) time you do something. But something my dad told me while I was learning to drive stuck me over the years: "Everyone was a new driver at some point."

And it's true. Everyone you see effortlessly driving on the streets and freeway today had their own Montgomery Ward's parking lot moment. Everyone you consider successful today had their initial bumps, rejections, stumbles and flat-out falls. In the movie *Selena*, about the successful and talented Tejano singer, a ten year old Selena Quintanilla and her siblings perform at the Harlingen State Fair to a lukewarm, almost nonexistent audience. The kids are feeling discouraged afterwards, and their father (also their manager) tells them: "Every star that's a star right now had their Harlingen once. And if we try hard and if we really want it...we can do it." Again, you are not failure as long as you have learned from your mistakes and experiences. In school as well as life, we often get better by trying, messing up, learning, and trying again and again.

If there's one thing I want you to take away from this book, it's that you get to keep on learning your entire life, and that's a good thing. It gives you the freedom to make mistakes, and do better. It gives you permission to stop beating yourself up, to stop putting unhelpful pressure on yourself to be an idealized or romanticized version of yourself. And it gives you the humility to become your authentic self.

Resources

Finding a Therapist

In-Person & Online Therapy:
OpenPath Collective:
WEBSITE: www.openpathcollective.org

Psychology Today's Find a Therapist Search Tool:
WEBSITE: www.psychologytoday.com/us/therapists

National Alliance on Mental Illness:
WEBSITE: www.nami.org
PHONE: 1-800-950-6264 (available 10AM-6PM EST, Monday-Friday)
NOTES: *provides therapy referrals and mental health resources*

S.A.F.E. (Self-Abuse Finally Ends) Alternatives:
WEBSITE: www.selfinjury.com
PHONE: 1-800-DONT-CUT
NOTES: *therapy referrals and resources focused on helping people stop self-harming behavior*

Substance Abuse & Mental Health Services Administration (SAMHSA) National Helpline:
WEBSITE: www.samhsa.gov
HELPLINE: 1-800-662-HELP (4357)

HELPLINE (FOR DEAF OR HARD OF HEARING): 1-800-487-4889
NOTES: *therapy referrals and resources for individuals and family members facing mental and/or substance use disorders*
Available 24/7/365

Online Therapy Platforms

BetterHelp: www.betterhelp.com
Talkspace: www.talkspace.com
Online-Therapy.com: www.online-therapy.com
MDLive: www.mdlive.com (therapy and psychiatry)
Pride Counseling: www.pridecounseling.com (LGBTQ focus)
Teen Counseling: www.teencounseling.com (serves ages 13-19)

Crisis Hotlines:

Crisis Text Line:
WEBSITE: **www.crisistextline.org**
TEXT HOME to 741741
Available 24/7/365
NOTES: provides free, confidential support via text message for anyone in emotional distress

National Suicide Prevention Lifeline:
WEBSITE: **www.suicidepreventionlifeline.org**
HOTLINE (ENGLISH): 1-800-273-8255
HOTLINE (EN ESPAÑOL): 1-888-628-9454
HOTLINE (FOR DEAF OR HARD OF HEARING): 1-800-799-4889
Available 24/7/365
NOTES: *provides free, confidential support to people in suicidal crisis or emotional distress*

Love Is Respect:
WEBSITE: www.loveisrespect.org
HOTLINE (English & Español): 1-866-331-9474
HOTLINE (for deaf or hard of hearing): 1-800-787-3224
TEXT LOVEIS to 1-866-331-9474
Available 24/7/365
NOTES: *offers confidential support for teens, young adults, and their loved ones seeking help, resources, or information related to healthy relationships and dating abuse in the US*

National Domestic Violence Hotline:
WEBSITE: www.thehotline.org
HOTLINE (ENGLISH & ESPAÑOL): 1-800-799-SAFE (7233)
HOTLINE (FOR DEAF OR HARD OF HEARING): 1-800-787-3224
Available 24/7/365
NOTES: *highly-trained, expert advocates offer free, confidential support, crisis intervention, education, and mental health referrals to survivors of domestic violence*

RAINN (Rape, Abuse & Incest National Network):
WEBSITE (ENGLISH): www.rainn.org
WEBSITE (ESPAÑOL): www.rainn.org/es
HOTLINE (ENGLISH & ESPAÑOL): 1-800-656-HOPE (4673)
HOTLINE (FOR DEAF OR HARD OF HEARING): 1-800-810-7440
Available 24/7/365
NOTES: *provides confidential support with a trained staff member from a sexual assault service provider in your area; can also provide therapy resources and referrals*

The Trevor Project:
WEBSITE: www.thetrevorproject.org
HOTLINE: 1-866-488-7386
TEXT START to 678678
Available 24/7/365
NOTES: *provides crisis intervention and suicide prevention services to lesbian, gay, bisexual, transgender, queer and questioning (LGBTQ) young people under 25*

Veterans Crisis Line:
WEBSITE: **www.veteranscrisisline.net**
HOTLINE: 1-800-273-TALK (8255) and press 1
TEXT 838255
Available 24/7/365
NOTES: *provides free, confidential crisis support for veterans, current service members, National Guard and Reserve members and their family and friends*

About the Author

Dr. Gina Davis is a licensed clinical psychologist in the San Francisco Bay Area. She previously worked at Mount St. Mary's University's Counseling & Psychological Services in Los Angeles as a Postdoctoral Fellow and as an Accessibility Specialist at the San Francisco Art Institute. Dr. Davis wrote her doctoral dissertation on the relationship between African American father involvement and the success of their college-age children, which she also presented at the Organization of Counseling Center Directors in Higher Education (OCCDHE) conference. She identifies as African American and Chinese American and as a person who stutters. Visit her online at www.ginadavispsyd.com.